go where you breathe free.

- butterflies rising -

Copyright © 2015-2022 butterflies rising

All rights reserved. All content of this book is original artistic work and protected by copyright law. All content included are original quotes, poems, and excerpts from previously published poems by butterflies rising. No part of this publication may be reproduced, distributed, or transmitted in any form or by any means. Content may not be attributed to someone else or credited as anyone else's work. Content also may not be used for any commercial purposes including, but not excluding, used on products, used in branding, reproduced, sold, or advertised in any manner.

Content may be shared in non-commercial use on digital platforms only with attribution to 'butterflies rising' included. Content may not be shared digitally or through any other medium without attribution to 'butterflies rising.'

ISBN: 978-0-578-37850-3 (Paperback)

butterfliesrising.com
butterfliesrisingpoetry.com
gowhereyoubreathefree.com

"go where you breathe free"

When I first wrote this quote, it came as a little message from the universe for me. For about 2 or 3 weeks, every morning when I was still in that not-quite-awake place, I kept hearing...

"go where you breathe free."

And it did speak to me about wild and free-spirited energy, nature, and adventure, but I also knew it was about more than just getting fresh air. I knew it was about all of the heavy and noisy energy in my life that was suffocating my spirit. And so I listened to it on a soul level.

I started searching for ways to help my soul breathe. Whether it was literally getting out in nature and breathing fresh air or untangling myself from energies in my life that held me back and going towards ones that took me closer to free. And I realize now that the messages that come from this quote and poem are something life will ask of me again and again. And I feel like others can understand and connect to those feelings, so I wanted to turn it all into an inspiration journal.

This little journal is filled with...

1. Blank pages and spaces for you to write out your own heart and soul
2. Some decorative nature scene pages where you can get a little creative and add in photos or small memory items
3. And then I've included a bunch of my quotes, poems, excerpts, and lines from poems that I've written and published over the years that all connect to or have to do with the different layers of meaning in *"go where you breathe free"* for me... little messages of free-spirited energy, nature, adventure, wild love... and little messages of spirit and soul.

So however this may speak to you, I just hope it's something that inspires you to *"go where you breathe free"*... whatever that means for your own soul.

that little
voice inside of you…
it's saying, *"go."* so just go.
go where you can
stretch out and reach
wide and high
and bloom wild and untamed
and be unapologetic in your essence
and reckless in your fire
and golden in your skin
and so. easy. in your breathing…
just. go.
to wherever the brutal voices quiet
and the aching doubt settles
and all those heavy fears you're holding
on to can start to loosen from your grip
and find little ways to fall away…
because that little voice… it's trying
to save your soul. so just go.
whatever it takes.
whatever you need to put down.
whatever you have to leave behind.
untangle from it all…
and *go where you breathe free.*

        - butterflies rising

go where you breathe free | butterflies rising

*i think it's breathtaking… how your
heart just spills out of you*

– butterflies rising

go where you breathe free | butterflies rising

*beautiful things spill out of you the way
wildfires burn… the way butterflies fly wild…
the way fireflies glow*

- butterflies rising

go where you breathe free | butterflies rising

go where you breathe free | butterflies rising

*just let your heart be fire and let your soul
be wild and let your spirit glow.*

– butterflies rising

go where you breathe free | butterflies rising

*patience with how your heart wanders…
you will find your way.*

- butterflies rising

go where you breathe free | butterflies rising

wild spirit, soft heart, sweet soul

- butterflies rising

go where you breathe free | butterflies rising

go where you breathe free | butterflies rising

*earth, fire, water, sky…
wild, soft, free… and full of flowers.
she makes everything beautiful,
everything about her is made of soul.*

- butterflies rising

go where you breathe free | butterflies rising

go where you breathe free | butterflies rising

*she's a flower out in the wilderness...
touched by moonlight and free in the
open air and wild sun*

- butterflies rising

go where you breathe free | butterflies rising

*in a wilderness,
with an unheld hand,
you will learn
to love yourself just as madly,
with the fierceness,
the recklessness,
that you have loved them*

- butterflies rising

go where you breathe free | butterflies rising

*there are
all those virgin,
unfelt things in you;
still untouched and tender
and unfolding...
so you have to keep searching...
for all that soul stuff*

- butterflies rising

go where you breathe free | butterflies rising

a soft lover... and a wild wanderer

- butterflies rising

go where you breathe free | butterflies rising

kissed by the sunlight and bitten by the moon

- butterflies rising

shadow & sugar…

you are
allowed to be
a many-layered thing…
to have texture and shades.
to be kissed by the sunlight
and bitten by the moon
and to feel all the different ways
that you feel,
all the raw and tender mess of it all.
to let all of that shadow and sugar be in you
and the pretty and dirty and beautiful and wild
run through you and spill out of you
everywhere, all at once…
to just let yourself be a soft and wild thing.

- butterflies rising

go where you breathe free | butterflies rising

you hold entire universes inside of you

– butterflies rising

go where you breathe free | butterflies rising

go where you breathe free | butterflies rising

go where you breathe free | butterflies rising

*if it needs you small, don't let it hold you anymore.
don't let anything that needs you ordinary
tame you ever again.*

      - butterflies rising

go where you breathe free | butterflies rising

what makes you feel...
what makes you. feel. alive.
how is your breath stolen.
how. and when.
does this life give you arrhythmia.
what pulls at you so much
that it hurts not to chase it.
the dreams out there, the hopes in here.
the art, the words, the songs... what shifts you.
that somewhere beautiful in this world
that calls to you in the early light.
those aching things that keep you up
so restless after midnight.
what takes you higher than this world,
what takes you deeper into your soul light...
all of those things...
i want to know. those. things...
show me all of your soul things

- butterflies rising

go where you breathe free | butterflies rising

go where you breathe free | butterflies rising

all
that destiny
in those wild eyes,
so much passion in
that wild heart,
all the marks on you
and the strength in you
from the mountains within you
that you've scaled to get here…
so. many. moons. in you
…*it's beautiful.*

- *butterflies rising*

go where you breathe free | butterflies rising

you have a breathtaking wildfire heart

- butterflies rising

go where you breathe free | butterflies rising

you've got
this big heart
and it's full of all
these big dreams
and maybe sometimes
they feel too big
and maybe sometimes
it feels too hard
but the heavens want to
have favor on you
and it may take a long time
but it will happen in its right time
so take a deep breath
and just hold on

- butterflies rising

go where you breathe free | butterflies rising

*please quiet the noise in my head
so i can hear the voice in my heart*

- butterflies rising

go where you breathe free | butterflies rising

go where you breathe free | butterflies rising

something like wings…

through all the
layers of dark and unsure
that wild in your heart
and those flowers in your chest
and the fire in your blood
and that feeling that you're going
to break. free. some. how.
have stirred within you
in spite of everything that has
tried to weigh heavy on your soul.
there's always been an ache in your back
that has felt something like wings…
something inside of you has always been
trying to carry you.

- *butterflies rising*

go where you breathe free | butterflies rising

go where you breathe free | butterflies rising

just hoping for gentle in the unknown

- butterflies rising

go where you breathe free | butterflies rising

*stretched out, wing tips touching
nothing but wild air*

- butterflies rising

go where you breathe free | butterflies rising

go where you breathe free | butterflies rising

my safe space…
is in the wild open.
where there's growing space
and soul-searching space,
and where my fire is bright,
and my wings are wide,
and my breathing
is all its own…
and where i can always feel the way
my heart beats on its own.

- *butterflies rising*

go where you breathe free | butterflies rising

she's a beautiful wildness on fire

- butterflies rising

she wanders
out in the flowers, in the wild,
where the breathing is easy and free...
because it's where the judgment goes quiet...
and everything beautiful is so untouched.
it's just beautiful. and wild. and fearless.
and whether it grows into something more
or burns down and has to start again,
it just does... fearlessly. beautifully. and wild.
so she wanders out where she can
learn to see herself that way;
to see herself in the way
that she looks at flowers...
like she's a beautiful wildness on fire.

- butterflies rising

go where you breathe free | butterflies rising

*the poetry
in those eyes…
those dreamer's eyes
learning to see in the dark.
and all that beautiful madness
tangled in your hair.
toes dangling over the edge,
testing a new universe...*

- butterflies rising

go where you breathe free | butterflies rising

*it's ok to take small steps and deep breaths, love…
but also, let yourself start to take up your space.
and don't you dare say you're sorry when you do.*

- butterflies rising

go where you breathe free | butterflies rising

*love me… and tell me how free my lungs
will always breathe when i love you.*

                    - butterflies rising

go where you breathe free | butterflies rising

*...i can get a little reckless
when my heart is restless*

- butterflies rising

go where you breathe free | butterflies rising

go where you breathe free | butterflies rising

he said,
do you want me here
close. soft with you.
or should i light it all up
and run wild with you?
i said... *yes.*

– *butterflies rising*

go where you breathe free | butterflies rising

Moonglow...

where the light falls and the beautiful stays,
when the stars settle in...
come with me.

- *butterflies rising*

go where you breathe free | butterflies rising

go where you breathe free | butterflies rising

*just take me somewhere that
takes my breath away*

— *butterflies rising*

go where you breathe free | butterflies rising

*go with me
everywhere in the world,
bare skin in sunshine,
wild under moonshine,
let's go*

- butterflies rising

go where you breathe free | butterflies rising

she gets wild with the moon and restless

- butterflies rising

go where you breathe free | butterflies rising

*...wild blossomed in the night
and searching for more
inside of herself*

- *butterflies rising*

go where you breathe free | butterflies rising

she's flower-sweet and fire-wild

- butterflies rising

go where you breathe free | butterflies rising

your wandering spirit
aching to find its way to open air,
searching for something golden
and sun-kissed,
reaching for so. much. more.
craving an untamed freedom
that tastes like pulse and heartbeat
and deep breath and wild skin.
and you feel it all. and you will find it.
because you're meant for it…
you've got all that wildflower energy
in your veins.

— *butterflies rising*

go where you breathe free | butterflies rising

*she's got all that
wildflower energy in her veins*

- butterflies rising

go where you breathe free | butterflies rising

go where you breathe free | butterflies rising

she's butterfly-wild, chasing all those inner fires, her restless spirit aching for something beautiful, reaching for something more

- butterflies rising

go where you breathe free | butterflies rising

go where you breathe free | butterflies rising

*she's always preferred sunrises over sunsets…
she likes beginnings*

– *butterflies rising*

go where you breathe free | butterflies rising

go where you breathe free | butterflies rising

there's something about the way dawn whispers
"so much is out there waiting"
that keeps my dreams breathing…

there's just a way that morning carries hope.

– *butterflies rising*

go where you breathe free | butterflies rising

go where you breathe free | butterflies rising

*may the sunrise bring you peace and
fill your soul with possibility*

- *butterflies rising*

go where you breathe free | butterflies rising

go where you breathe free | butterflies rising

this becoming
will ask for your breath,
patience
and for your fight,
perseverance

transformation is made of
both surrender and strength

- *butterflies rising*

go where you breathe free | butterflies rising

the first step in setting yourself free…
i am willing to grow.

- butterflies rising

go where you breathe free | butterflies rising

let a new version of you be uncovered

– butterflies rising

go where you breathe free | butterflies rising

go where you breathe free | butterflies rising

*grace…
learning to let things be
not meant for me*

- butterflies rising

go where you breathe free | butterflies rising

breathe easy now…
you don't have to carry other
people's heavy anymore

- butterflies rising

go where you breathe free | butterflies rising

go where you breathe free | butterflies rising

*take time
to cleanse,
to heal,
to renew,
to grow,
to become.*

- butterflies rising

go where you breathe free | butterflies rising

write it out until what hurt you heals

- butterflies rising

this is a growing season,
of change, of turning, of shedding,
of letting things fall away,
and fall apart, and come undone,
and be uncovered

and then a space of surrender,
and being, just being.

and the reflections here are temporary,
so take them in and honor them,
and be honest with them, and own
them…but then forgive them,
and don't stay in them

let it all go… *let yourself bloom.*

- butterflies rising

go where you breathe free | butterflies rising

go where you breathe free | butterflies rising

go where you breathe free | butterflies rising

let it all go... let yourself bloom.

– butterflies rising

go where you breathe free | butterflies rising

go where you breathe free | butterflies rising

*let the
wonder and beauty
of your existence
fall out of you
everywhere, unafraid
no matter who may take it in
or hold it with care
let it all be
unshaken by the cold*

- butterflies rising

go where you breathe free | butterflies rising

beautiful
wildflower…
be free and reach
for the sun,
live in all your
colors and grow
so untamed

– *butterflies rising*

go where you breathe free | butterflies rising

beautiful wildflower, grow untamed

- butterflies rising

go where you breathe free | butterflies rising

go where you breathe free | butterflies rising

lay here...
safe in the morning light,
soft in the daylight,
until sunlight becomes skin light,
breathe in and let the flowers
wrap you up in sweet until the air comes
easy from your chest,
until the sky becomes something you can touch,
and the earth becomes somewhere you can stay
and still have wings

- *butterflies rising*

go where you breathe free | butterflies rising

go where you breathe free | butterflies rising

*unfolding into yourself…
what a tender, delicate thing*

- butterflies rising

go where you breathe free | butterflies rising

*on your own
is where your
wildflowers grow,
there's no one else here to
block their sun,
but no one else can water
them but you*

- butterflies rising

go where you breathe free | butterflies rising

i've been letting go of heavy things

- butterflies rising

go where you breathe free | butterflies rising

go where you breathe free | butterflies rising

i've been healing
a spirit, and tending to a soul, and
listening to a heart. and i've started to
exhale. and to breathe in… and to
breathe. in. a life

– *butterflies rising*

go where you breathe free | butterflies rising

*what your heart can't settle…
just give it to the universe*

- butterflies rising

go where you breathe free | butterflies rising

...to just let it all be unheavy

– butterflies rising

go where you breathe free | butterflies rising

go where you breathe free | butterflies rising

we heal
we grow
we become full
we rise
we thrive
and we fly

- butterflies rising

go where you breathe free | butterflies rising

go where you breathe free | butterflies rising

The Turning Point...

let go your fear
as it falls
beautiful, be still
this untangling of it all
let your bones fill with might
let your lungs fill with free

don't look back.

    - butterflies rising

go where you breathe free | butterflies rising

*who are you when you let the
things you fear fall away...*

- butterflies rising

go where you breathe free | butterflies rising

let's lose ourselves in wild creativity

– butterflies rising

go where you breathe free | butterflies rising

go where you breathe free | butterflies rising

*meet me where we can
lose ourselves in the wild and feel it all…
burn and breathe at once
in our skin.
out of our lungs.
pouring the aches from our chests,
with our wings wide open.*

- butterflies rising

go where you breathe free | butterflies rising

go where you breathe free | butterflies rising

we burn, we run, we love

- butterflies rising

go where you breathe free | butterflies rising

*some people's very existence
inspires you to dream*

- butterflies rising

go where you breathe free | butterflies rising

*i want to fall
into that beautiful life
into the soft spaces
into the glow
where there's moonlight
where there's soul light
and where it means something
if you come close
and let your heart beat
against mine*

- butterflies rising

go where you breathe free | butterflies rising

go where you breathe free | butterflies rising

how you look at
me makes me wonder...
where do i belong if not right here.
right next to you.
breathing in all the life
under these stars until
this world ends

   - *butterflies rising*

go where you breathe free | butterflies rising

go where you breathe free | butterflies rising

burn out the stars with me

– butterflies rising

go where you breathe free | butterflies rising

go where you breathe free | butterflies rising

some people are just light, glow, hope… human stars.

– butterflies rising

go where you breathe free | butterflies rising

she blooms wild and burns bright

- butterflies rising

go where you breathe free | butterflies rising

go where you breathe free | butterflies rising

under the sun
is where her flowers bloom,
under the moon
is where her fires burn,
out in the wild
is where her spirit breathes…
she's meant to be wild,
so beautifully wild.

- butterflies rising

go where you breathe free | butterflies rising

she's a wildflower on fire

- butterflies rising

she's a
wildflower on fire
with all that sweet soul sugar
and an ache inside to unfold
and to grow into so much more,
all that destiny written in her eyes,
she's wild butterflies,
and she feels her heart pulled
under the wild of the moon to face her
fears and to find her way through all of
the dark and the heavy that she's
carried for so long…there's fight here,
but there's surrender here too.
and there could be so much freedom here
if she could just let herself fall into
that beautiful chaos and dig deep into that
passion in her bones…
she could uncover all the beautiful things
that those wildfires inside of her hold.

- *butterflies rising*

go where you breathe free | butterflies rising

go where you breathe free | butterflies rising

*this is a growing season...
so bloom wild and untamed*

- butterflies rising

go where you breathe free | butterflies rising

i can feel it…
how i'm on my way,
to somewhere different,
something better than this

and i'll let it be light, and new,
and undiscovered

- *butterflies rising*

go where you breathe free | butterflies rising

go where you breathe free | butterflies rising

*your heart
isn't made to settle…
you must choose the greatest love,
and you have to chase the
greatest life*

- butterflies rising

go where you breathe free | butterflies rising

go where you breathe free | butterflies rising

you'll be rejected
for these wings, these fires,
for this sweet and wild rebellion in you.
but these are such. beautiful. things.
so keep choosing you…
because nothing will matter
if you reject you.

– *butterflies rising*

go where you breathe free | butterflies rising

*keep chasing all that sweet and
wild rebellion in you*

- butterflies rising

go where you breathe free | butterflies rising

don't be afraid
to leave it all behind…
there is new light, and new life,
there are new worlds waiting

- *butterflies rising*

go where you breathe free | butterflies rising

go where you breathe free | butterflies rising

go where you breathe free | butterflies rising

*...let it all fall through your fingers
until you feel free*

-butterflies rising

go where you breathe free | butterflies rising

exit gracefully.
heal and grow.
don't look back.

– butterflies rising

go where you breathe free | butterflies rising

go where you breathe free | butterflies rising

*dream
your wild dreams, love,
and chase your racing heartbeats*

- butterflies rising

go where you breathe free | butterflies rising

keep your heart wilder than wild

- butterflies rising

go where you breathe free | butterflies rising

you make sure
you keep loving deep.
and *keep your heart wilder than wild,*
because someday you'll
breathe it all out as stardust and art…

– *butterflies rising*

go where you breathe free | butterflies rising

go where you breathe free | butterflies rising

exhale it all as stardust and art

- butterflies rising

i want…
to search. and stretch.
and grow. and glow.
and drip myself in wild creativity,
and burn and breathe at once
in this skin. in these lungs.
wings untethered,
under the moon, into the sky,
and to dream big and bigger and biggest,
and to feel free in here…
inside my anxious chest.
to just. feel. free.
and to have the universe
say… *yes*, you are worthy of all this.

        - *butterflies rising*

go where you breathe free | butterflies rising

like a butterfly, her wings unfolded

- butterflies rising

go where you breathe free | butterflies rising

go where you breathe free | butterflies rising

there she was… so beautiful and free

– butterflies rising

go where you breathe free | butterflies rising

go where you breathe free | butterflies rising

you said,
tell me where you've been, love

and i thought of all the lost roads,
and dark corners,

and heavy work, and heartbreak,
and of all the healing

and i just said…
on my way here

– *butterflies rising*

go where you breathe free | butterflies rising

go where you breathe free | butterflies rising

go where you breathe free | butterflies rising

*your beating heart, wild air, and
all the other things that make
me want to run free*

- butterflies rising

go where you breathe free | butterflies rising

*the world is loud...
and i wanna get lost with you*

— *butterflies rising*

go where you breathe free | butterflies rising

playlist in the background, stars outside the windows… let's just drive.

- butterflies rising

go where you breathe free | butterflies rising

Road Trip...

just give me
your young, wild heart,
and i'll give you
my young, wild heart,
and we'll light up every city
and burn through every town
with how it feels

— *butterflies rising*

go where you breathe free | butterflies rising

let go, run wild with me

– butterflies rising

go where you breathe free | butterflies rising

we have
wilderness hearts,
we get restless with the moon,
we're meant to live in wild opens,
and run free under
starlight

– *butterflies rising*

go where you breathe free | butterflies rising

go where you breathe free | butterflies rising

let's run free under starlight

- *butterflies rising*

go where you breathe free | butterflies rising

*let's run free under starlight…
we'll leave all of our doubts behind us
where they came from,
and we'll believe. so. much. that we just can't
be told different… restless for our dreams
and full of wild defiance*

- butterflies rising

go where you breathe free | butterflies rising

*if it keeps your heart restless and aching
to touch stars… then i hope you stay dreaming
for it, i hope you hold on.*

- butterflies rising

go where you breathe free | butterflies rising

if it keeps you up at 3am,
i hope you're cultivating worth,
and nurturing patience, and building pathways
that you find your way to in the sunlight

— *purpose*

- *butterflies rising*

go where you breathe free | butterflies rising

go where you breathe free | butterflies rising

we crave a soul-stirring love and
we chase that soul-stirring life

- butterflies rising

go where you breathe free | butterflies rising

go where you breathe free | butterflies rising

meet me in that place
where our souls ache to wander
and a million stars will unfold around us
and i'll look at you and wonder
how we ever lived in anything
less breathtaking
than this

— *butterflies rising*

go where you breathe free | butterflies rising

go where you breathe free | butterflies rising

let's go where everything is soft and wild...
give me love like flowers and fire

- butterflies rising

go where you breathe free | butterflies rising

go where you breathe free | butterflies rising

she's flowers and fire

- butterflies rising

go where you breathe free | butterflies rising

*to be such a soft thing…
and still let everything made of fire
run so wild in your veins*

- butterflies rising

go where you breathe free | butterflies rising

*you are a wild thing…
but you are such a tender thing*

- *butterflies rising*

passion.
and vulnerability.
fire and wild and art and love
and sugar and soul.
a pull towards the stars;
an ache to be more free…
to feel. so. alive.
with a need to feel things deeper
and sweeter and closer,
and a heart that changes shape
when something moves you.
it's all so beautiful.
so let go of the ways this
world says you're supposed to be
and feel all of the ways
that your soul is.

– *butterflies rising*

go where you breathe free | butterflies rising

she's beautiful chaos and wild butterflies

- butterflies rising

go where you breathe free | butterflies rising

go where you breathe free | butterflies rising

let yourself be a many-layered thing

- butterflies rising

go where you breathe free | butterflies rising

go where you breathe free | butterflies rising

i like you brave,
i like you breathing free,
i like you feeling all of you in you

— *butterflies rising*

go where you breathe free | butterflies rising

go where you breathe free | butterflies rising

tell me how
the mountains give you peace
and the ocean makes you restless,
of the poetry you read
and the song you fall asleep with,
any fear that makes you bleed
and every dream that breaks you open,
this is what i want to know,
this is how my heart falls

— *butterflies rising*

go where you breathe free | butterflies rising

go where you breathe free | butterflies rising

go where you breathe free | butterflies rising

*i'm restless and wild again…
and all i wanna do is get
lost with you.*

- butterflies rising

go where you breathe free | butterflies rising

go where you breathe free | butterflies rising

A Wild Open...

love me in a wild open
with a gentle hold
where i find myself, in myself
but let me feel
your racing heart
and your burning blood
through your steady hands
and let this be how we love
so we can love in a way that the stars
we come from want for us to know

let us burn and breathe all at once

- *butterflies rising*

go where you breathe free | butterflies rising

*you and i…
we're meant to live in wild opens*

- butterflies rising

go where you breathe free | butterflies rising

*meet me where moonlight meets soul light
and everything we both ache for collides*

- butterflies rising

go where you breathe free | butterflies rising

go where you breathe free | butterflies rising

summer air, freedom, and you

- butterflies rising

go where you breathe free | butterflies rising

go where you breathe free | butterflies rising

*let me
wander with the ones
who are tangled in stars
and tethered to promise*

- dreamers

- butterflies rising

go where you breathe free | butterflies rising

*why else are we here if not to live with
unreasonable passion for things*

- butterflies rising

go where you breathe free | butterflies rising

go where you breathe free | butterflies rising

passion in my chest like kerosene

– butterflies rising

go where you breathe free | butterflies rising

what if the
raging inside of you
is something beautiful…
your curiosity stretching
and your soul stirring…
all that wildflower energy in your veins.
and the ache is everything you've suffocated
for so long just trying to find some way to breathe.
and when it feels like you're burning it all down,
you're just still learning how to burn bright.
maybe you go a little wayward
and get a little reckless,
but be easy on your restless heart;
have a little grace with your fire…
you're a wild butterfly finding your way,
just a girl growing wings.

- *butterflies rising*

go where you breathe free | butterflies rising

go where you breathe free | butterflies rising

she's a wild butterfly finding her way

- butterflies rising

go where you breathe free | butterflies rising

go where you breathe free | butterflies rising

just a girl growing wings

- butterflies rising

go where you breathe free | butterflies rising

go where you breathe free | butterflies rising

there is this
stunning breathing rhythm
in a woman learning to love herself

this slow rise as she feels her way into
every inch of her skin like honey,
and this soft fall as she settles into grace

this is the breath i seek

— *butterflies rising*

go where you breathe free | butterflies rising

go where you breathe free | butterflies rising

go where you breathe free | butterflies rising

*to be steady in the soul
and free in the spirit*

- butterflies rising

go where you breathe free | butterflies rising

these soft, quiet, intimate moments
that your heart is beating are precious,
so if it takes you out of your peace...
don't give it your little moments

- butterflies rising

go where you breathe free | butterflies rising

go where you breathe free | butterflies rising

*just breathe...
and stay here in your peace*

- butterflies rising

go where you breathe free | butterflies rising

go where you breathe free | butterflies rising

*let your head quiet,
go where your heart sways*

- butterflies rising

go where you breathe free | butterflies rising

*your heart tells you big things
in little ways… listen.*

- butterflies rising

go where you breathe free | butterflies rising

feel
everything
that is
beautiful and possible
in your soul,
and let yourself
become it

– *butterflies rising*

go where you breathe free | butterflies rising

go where you breathe free | butterflies rising

*if this life doesn't look like your
soul feels, keep going.*

- *butterflies rising*

go where you breathe free | butterflies rising

you have to keep going.
there are wilder sunsets and more colors to know.
and there are still answers for what's pulling at you.
and i think you have to chase them…
i think you have to keep going.

- *butterflies rising*

go where you breathe free | butterflies rising

go where you can
stretch out and reach
wide and high
and bloom wild and untamed
and be unapologetic in your essence
and reckless in your fire
and golden in your skin
and so. easy. in your breathing…
just. go.

go where you breathe free.

- butterflies rising

go where you breathe free | butterflies rising

go where you breathe free | butterflies rising

go where you breathe free

– butterflies rising

go where you breathe free | butterflies rising

go where you breathe free | butterflies rising

Made in the USA
Coppell, TX
29 December 2023

27012529R00125